THIS BOOK WAS CREATED AS A RESULT OF YEARS STANDING BESIDE FAMILIES AS THEY EXPERIENCED THE LOSS OF A CHILD. THIS BOOK IS INTENDED TO BRING COMFORT TO THE CHILDREN THAT ARE ALSO AFFECTED. IT INCLUDES A LOT OF PRAYERS AND GOD'S GRACE.

ILLUSTRATIONS BY: CREATIVEVALUATION

I HAVE A
brother
IN HEAVEN

WRITTEN BY
AUTUMN DOAN

ILLUSTRATED BY
CREATIVEVALUATION

2 CORINTHIANS 1: 3-5

TAKE HEART, MY CHILD.
FOR HE HOLDS US.

CLOSELY & DEARLY.

Dear reader,

As you read this book it is important for you to know that having a lot of questions and feelings about having a brother in heaven is okay. We may talk about some things that sound different than you may have heard before. You may have more questions to ask once we are through. It is my wish for you that you can feel comfortable asking God about all these things. He talks to us and helps us when we don't even know it sometimes. He is a good God even when we can't understand why he allows bad things to happen. He knows you and he knows your brother. Trust in Him always and He will keep you safe.

Autumn

I HAVE A BROTHER IN HEAVEN.

I KNOW THIS BECAUSE MY MOTHER TOLD ME SO. EXCEPT, I DON'T REALLY UNDERSTAND WHAT THIS MEANS. I JUST TELL PEOPLE THAT IS WHERE HE LIVES AND THEY USUALLY DON'T ASK ME ANY MORE ABOUT IT.

DAD SAID IT MEANS THAT MY LITTLE BROTHER COULDN'T STAY HERE WITH US BECAUSE GOD WANTED HIM TO BE WITH HIM. THAT DOESN'T SEEM VERY FAIR TO ME, BUT NOBODY ASKED ME ANYWAY.

SOMETIMES WE TALK ABOUT MY BROTHER AND WE EVEN EAT CAKE ON HIS BIRTHDAY. IT CONFUSES ME BECAUSE HE CAN'T EAT IT, CAN HE? DOES HE GET OLDER EVERY YEAR LIKE ME?

I HAVE A LOT OF QUESTIONS BUT I DON'T REALLY ASK THEM BECAUSE SOMETIMES IT MAKES MOMMY AND DADDY SAD, OR THEY DON'T KNOW THE ANSWER. I KNOW THEY LOVE HIM AND MISS HIM VERY MUCH. I DON'T WANT TO MAKE THEM SAD.

CAN YOU HELP ME UNDERSTAND?

WHY DID MY BROTHER GO TO HEAVEN?

WHY DID MY BROTHER GO TO HEAVEN?

MY SWEET CHILD. THIS MAY JUST BE THE HARDEST QUESTION TO ANSWER. I WILL TRY MY BEST FOR YOU.

YOUR BROTHER DIDN'T DO ANYTHING WRONG. HE WASN'T SENT AWAY TO LIVE IN A FARAWAY PLACE BECAUSE HE WAS IN TROUBLE, AND HE WOULD PROBABLY HAVE LOVED TO STAY AND PLAY WITH YOU HERE. WE HAVE A FATHER IN HEAVEN, NAMED GOD, AND HE LOVES US ALL. HE IS A VERY GOOD FATHER. LOVING AND KIND. HE PROTECTS US AND HELPS US DO THE RIGHT THINGS. BUT, SOMETIMES, INSTEAD OF US LIVING HERE, HE CALLS US TO HIS HOUSE. THAT IS CALLED HEAVEN. IT IS SUCH A HAPPY PLACE AND NOBODY EVEN CRIES WHEN THEY ARE THERE. ONE DAY WE WILL GET TO SEE IT BUT NOT UNTIL HE CALLS US TO COME.

HAVE YOU EVER HAD TO GO SOMEWHERE YOU WEREN'T
REALLY SURE ABOUT WITH YOUR PARENTS, BUT THEN WHEN
YOU GOT THERE YOU REALLY LIKED IT?

THIS IS WHY YOUR BROTHER HAD TO GO TO HEAVEN. OUR
HEAVENLY FATHER, GOD, ASKED HIM TO.

WHERE IS HEAVEN?

WHERE IS HEAVEN?

OH, I AM TOLD HEAVEN IS WONDERFUL! IT IS WHERE GOD
LIVES. SOME PEOPLE TELL YOU IT IS WAY, WAY HIGH IN THE
SKY, PAST THE CLOUDS AND EVEN FARTHER THAN OUTER
SPACE. SO FAR AWAY THAT WE CAN'T SEE IT.

ANGELS LIVE IN HEAVEN, TOO. HAVE YOU EVER HEARD OF
ANGELS? THERE ARE A LOT OF THEM. WHAT A COOL
THOUGHT TO THINK YOUR BROTHER IS LIVING IN HEAVEN
WITH GOD AND ALL THE ANGELS.

YOU KNOW, IF YOU WANTED TO, YOU COULD GO OUTSIDE
AND LOOK AT THE BIG SKY AND IMAGINE HOW FAR AWAY
HEAVEN IS. YOU COULD EVEN IMAGINE YOURSELF FLYING SO
HIGH THAT YOUR WINGS WOULD GET TIRED BEFORE YOU
COULD GET EVEN AS FAR AS SPACE. BUT, DON'T WORRY,
BECAUSE YOUR BROTHER DIDN'T GET TIRED. GOD GAVE HIM
A RIDE AND HE MADE IT JUST FINE.

WHY COULDN'T MY BROTHER
STAY HERE WITH ME?

WHY COULDN'T MY BROTHER STAY HERE WITH ME?

I BET YOU WOULD HAVE BEEN THE BEST OF FRIENDS! PROBABLY EVEN HAD A FEW GOOD SIBLING FIGHTS, TOO - BUT MOSTLY FRIENDS. IT DOESN'T SEEM VERY FAIR, DOES IT, THAT GOD WOULD TAKE HIM FROM HERE?

DO YOU THINK GOD WAS BEING MEAN OR SELFISH?

I KNOW THAT WHEN SOMEONE TAKES SOMETHING AWAY FROM US IT SEEMS VERY RUDE AND NOT VERY FRIENDLY AT ALL. WE EVEN GET IN TROUBLE FOR IT SOMETIMES. IN TIMES LIKE THESE, YOU HAVE TO REMEMBER HOW MUCH GOD LOVES YOU. HE WOULD NEVER BE MEAN TO YOU. HE LOVES YOU SO DEARLY THAT IT IS HARD FOR EVEN THE SMARTEST PERSON IN THE WHOLE WORLD TO EXPLAIN. BUT, YES, I CAN SEE WHERE IT FEELS MEAN BECAUSE IT MAKES YOU SO SAD.

DARLING CHILD, I WANT TO TELL YOU THAT YOU CAN ASK
GOD ABOUT THIS. HE MIGHT NOT ANSWER YOU RIGHT AWAY
BUT I KNOW HE HEARS YOU AND WILL GIVE YOU GREAT BIG
HUGS FROM HEAVEN UNTIL THEN. JUST CLOSE YOUR EYES
AND IMAGINE HIM HUGGING YOU NOW!

SHOULD WE CELEBRATE HIS BIRTHDAY?

SHOULD WE CELEBRATE HIS BIRTHDAY?

EVERY FAMILY IS DIFFERENT. WE ALL LIKE TO CELEBRATE BIRTHDAYS AND HOLIDAYS DIFFERENTLY. THAT IS OKAY! IT MAY SEEM STRANGE TO HAVE A BIRTHDAY CAKE OR CELEBRATION FOR YOUR BROTHER WHEN HE ISN'T HERE, BUT IT IS MEANT TO BE A HAPPY THING. IT IS A TIME TO REMEMBER HOW MUCH YOUR BROTHER MEANS TO YOUR FAMILY. EVEN THOUGH HE CAN'T HAVE CAKE WITH YOU, YOUR FAMILY GETS TO HAVE A SPECIAL MOMENT EVERY YEAR JUST TO REMEMBER HIM.

DO YOU LIKE TO BE REMEMBERED ON YOUR BIRTHDAY? I BET YOU DO! I ALSO BET YOUR FAVORITE PART IS THE PRESENTS.

HE DOESN'T GET OLDER EACH YEAR, BUT DID YOU KNOW YOUR BROTHER GOT THE BEST PRESENT ANYONE COULD HAVE EVER GAVE HIM? HE GOT TO GO TO HEAVEN WITH GOD!

IT IS OKAY TO HAVE SPECIAL MOMENTS FOR PEOPLE WE MISS. IT MAKES OUR HEARTS A LITTLE SAD BUT HAPPY AT THE SAME TIME. IT IS AN EXPRESSION OF LOVE.

CAN I HELP MOMMY AND
DADDY TO NOT BE SO SAD?

CAN I HELP MOMMY AND DADDY TO NOT BE SO SAD?

YES, YOU CAN! YOU ARE PROBABLY THE THING THAT MAKES THEM THE MOST HAPPY. DID YOU KNOW THAT? DID YOU KNOW THAT WHEN YOU GIVE THEM HUGS AND SNUGGLE THEM TIGHT, YOU ARE GIVING THEM A LOT OF LOVE? WHEN YOU ARE HELPFUL WITH CHORES AND PICKING UP YOUR THINGS, THAT IS GOOD TOO. MOMS AND DADS EVEN LIKE TO TALK WITH YOU ABOUT YOUR BROTHER AND ANSWER ANY QUESTIONS YOU MIGHT HAVE. THEY LIKE THAT YOU LOVE HIM, TOO.

SOMETIMES WE THINK THAT IT IS BETTER NOT TO TALK ABOUT THESE THINGS, BUT I THINK IT IS VERY HELPFUL WHEN WE DO. ONE OR ALL OF YOU MAY CRY, BUT THAT IS OKAY. YOU CAN CRY TOGETHER AND BE LIKE THE ELEPHANTS.

YES, I SAID ELEPHANTS! DID YOU KNOW ELEPHANTS ARE VERY
CARING AND HELPFUL TO EACH OTHER WHEN ANOTHER
ELEPHANT DIES? ESPECIALLY THE BABIES. THEY SUPPORT
EACH OTHER AND THEY REMEMBER LIKE WE DO. THEY ARE A
FAMILY AND WE ALWAYS HELP OUR FAMILY.

IS IT WEIRD TO TALK ABOUT HIM WITH MY FRIENDS?

IS IT WEIRD TO TALK ABOUT HIM WITH MY FRIENDS?

THERE IS NOTHING WRONG WITH TALKING ABOUT YOUR BROTHER WITH YOUR FRIENDS. AT FIRST THEY MAY HAVE A LOT OF QUESTIONS AND SOME MAY NOT REALLY UNDERSTAND WHAT HAPPENED, BUT IT IS STILL OKAY TO TALK TO THEM ABOUT HIM. HE IS A PART OF YOU.

IF THERE ARE DAYS YOU FEEL SAD BECAUSE YOU MISS HIM, ASK A FRIEND TO TALK TO YOU ABOUT IT. IF SOMETHING REMINDS YOU OF HIM WHEN YOU ARE PLAYING, OR IN CLASS, IT IS OKAY TO SAY SO.

I ALSO WANT YOU TO KNOW THAT IF YOU ARE NOT COMFORTABLE TALKING TO YOUR FRIENDS OR OTHERS ABOUT HIM, THAT IS OKAY TOO.

YOU ARE NOT WEIRD.

ONE LAST THOUGHT.

WHAT A SPECIAL CHILD YOU ARE. I CAN TELL FROM HERE.

I HOPE I HAVE ANSWERED SOME OF YOUR QUESTIONS FOR YOU. I KNOW YOU LOVE YOUR BROTHER VERY MUCH. I ALSO HOPE YOU KNOW THAT NOBODY DID ANYTHING WRONG AND ONE DAY YOU WILL GET TO MEET HIM AGAIN - WHEN YOU GET TO GO TO HEAVEN. DON'T RUSH IT THOUGH! THERE IS STILL A LOT TO DO HERE. GOD NEEDS YOUR HELP IN HIS ARMY!

ARMY? OH THAT IS A WHOLE OTHER CONVERSATION THAT WE CAN HAVE ONE DAY.

I PRAY THAT GOD TALKS TO YOU ALL THE TIME AND YOU TALK TO HIM. THAT HE HELPS YOU UNDERSTAND HIS LOVE, AND THAT YOU, MY SWEET, SWEET, CHILD, LOOK TO HIM FOR ALL YOUR ANSWERS IN LIFE. READING HIS BIBLE IS A GOOD PLACE TO START.

DEAR PARENTS.

I AM VERY SORRY THAT THIS IS A BOOK YOU ARE READING, OR
SHARING WITH A CHILD. MY HEART GOES OUT TO YOU BECAUSE
I KNOW THAT YOUR HEART ACHES AND YOU HAVE QUESTIONS
OF YOUR OWN. I HAVE STOOD BESIDE FAMILIES FOR THE LAST
SEVEN YEARS HOLDING THEIR HANDS IN THE TOUGHEST
MOMENTS OF THEIR LIFE. I HAVE FOUND THAT EVEN THOUGH
WE DON'T ALWAYS GET THE ANSWERS WE WANT, GOD DOES
SHOW UP AND HOLD US TIGHT. THE GRIEF AND ANGER CAN SET
IN SO STRONG THAT IT IS HARD TO FEEL HIM SOMETIMES, BUT
REST ASSURED, HE WILL NOT LEAVE YOU. IT IS OKAY TO HAVE
THESE EMOTIONS, JUST LIKE IT IS OKAY FOR OTHER MEMBERS OF
YOUR FAMILY TO FEEL THEM, TOO. YOU ARE STRONGER
TOGETHER AND YOU WILL FOREVER SHARE THE BOND OF
KNOWING HIM. RELY ON ONE ANOTHER. LET YOUR HUGS
MOVE MOUNTAINS AND YOUR TEARS FILL RIVERS. IT IS ALL JUST
YOUR LOVE FOR HIM FLOWING FROM YOUR HEARTS, SEEKING A
PLACE TO REST AND NOURISH SOMETHING MORE. DO WHAT
FEELS RIGHT TO YOU. THERE IS NOTHING WRONG WITH TAKING
MOMENTS TO REMEMBER HIM. TO ASK OTHERS TO JOIN YOU.
TALKING ABOUT HIM AND TELLING OTHERS OF HIM IS
PERFECTLY FINE. MORE THAN FINE.

I KNOW IT SOUNDS CLICHÉ, BUT TRUST THAT YOU ARE NOT
ALONE. MILLIONS OF PARENTS AROUND THE WORLD HAVE
ACHING HEARTS JUST LIKE YOURS. REACH OUT. ALLOW
CONVERSATIONS AND LET OTHERS KNOW HOW MUCH YOU
LOVE HIM. GOD WORKS THROUGH OTHERS.

I KEEP YOU IN MY PRAYERS. THAT GOD WILL HOLD YOU CLOSE,
YOU WILL HAVE GRACE AND THAT HE GUIDES YOUR HEART.

Printed in Great Britain
by Amazon

45158339R00023